Go and Get It!

Jane Langford

Illustrated by Teri Gower

Our dog Spike
had a big stick.
He wanted to play with it.

"Spike, go and get the stick!" shouted Dad.

Spike had a tennis ball.
He wanted to play with it.

"Go and get the tennis ball!" shouted Dad to Spike.

Spike had a rubber bone.
He wanted to play with it.

"Go and get the bone Spike!" shouted Dad.

Then Spike saw a cat.
He wanted to play with it.

"Go and get the dog!" shouted Mum to Dad.